DETAILS

Company Name	
Company Reg	
Address	
E-mail	
Phone Number	
Fax Number	

LOG BOOK DETAILS

Log Start Date	
Log End Date	
Log Book No.	

NOTES

Dedication

This Visitor Log Book is dedicated to all the businesses out there who want to keep their visitor notes organized and document their findings in the process.

You are my inspiration for producing books and I'm honored to be a part of keeping all of your visitor notes and records organized.

This journal notebook will help you record the details of who is coming in and who is going out.

Thoughtfully put together with these sections to record: Company Contact Details, Log Book Details, Visitor Log.

How to Use this Book

The purpose of this book is to keep all of your Visitor Log Book notes all in one place. It will help keep you organized.

This Visitor Log Book will allow you to accurately document details about people coming in and people going out.

 Here are examples of the prompts for you to fill in and write about your experience in this book:

1. Company Contact Details - Write Company Name, Company Reg, Address, Email, Phone Number, Fax Number.

2. Log Book Details - Write Log Start Date, Log End Date, Log Book Number, Notes.

3. Visitor Log - Record Day, Name, To See, Time In, and Time Out.

VISITOR LOG

DAY	NAME	TO SEE	TIME IN	TIME OUT

VISITOR LOG

DAY	NAME	TO SEE	TIME IN	TIME OUT

VISITOR LOG

DAY	NAME	TO SEE	TIME IN	TIME OUT

VISITOR LOG

DAY	NAME	TO SEE	TIME IN	TIME OUT

VISITOR LOG

DAY	NAME	TO SEE	TIME IN	TIME OUT

VISITOR LOG

DAY	NAME	TO SEE	TIME IN	TIME OUT

VISITOR LOG

DAY	NAME	TO SEE	TIME IN	TIME OUT

VISITOR LOG

DAY	NAME	TO SEE	TIME IN	TIME OUT

VISITOR LOG

DAY	NAME	TO SEE	TIME IN	TIME OUT

VISITOR LOG

DAY	NAME	TO SEE	TIME IN	TIME OUT

VISITOR LOG

DAY	NAME	TO SEE	TIME IN	TIME OUT

VISITOR LOG

DAY	NAME	TO SEE	TIME IN	TIME OUT

VISITOR LOG

DAY	NAME	TO SEE	TIME IN	TIME OUT

VISITOR LOG

DAY	NAME	TO SEE	TIME IN	TIME OUT

VISITOR LOG

DAY	NAME	TO SEE	TIME IN	TIME OUT

VISITOR LOG

DAY	NAME	TO SEE	TIME IN	TIME OUT

VISITOR LOG

DAY	NAME	TO SEE	TIME IN	TIME OUT

VISITOR LOG

DAY	NAME	TO SEE	TIME IN	TIME OUT

VISITOR LOG

DAY	NAME	TO SEE	TIME IN	TIME OUT

VISITOR LOG

DAY	NAME	TO SEE	TIME IN	TIME OUT

VISITOR LOG

DAY	NAME	TO SEE	TIME IN	TIME OUT

VISITOR LOG

DAY	NAME	TO SEE	TIME IN	TIME OUT

VISITOR LOG

DAY	NAME	TO SEE	TIME IN	TIME OUT

VISITOR LOG

DAY	NAME	TO SEE	TIME IN	TIME OUT

VISITOR LOG

DAY	NAME	TO SEE	TIME IN	TIME OUT

VISITOR LOG

DAY	NAME	TO SEE	TIME IN	TIME OUT

VISITOR LOG

DAY	NAME	TO SEE	TIME IN	TIME OUT

VISITOR LOG

DAY	NAME	TO SEE	TIME IN	TIME OUT

VISITOR LOG

DAY	NAME	TO SEE	TIME IN	TIME OUT

VISITOR LOG

DAY	NAME	TO SEE	TIME IN	TIME OUT

VISITOR LOG

DAY	NAME	TO SEE	TIME IN	TIME OUT

VISITOR LOG

DAY	NAME	TO SEE	TIME IN	TIME OUT

VISITOR LOG

DAY	NAME	TO SEE	TIME IN	TIME OUT

VISITOR LOG

DAY	NAME	TO SEE	TIME IN	TIME OUT

VISITOR LOG

DAY	NAME	TO SEE	TIME IN	TIME OUT

VISITOR LOG

DAY	NAME	TO SEE	TIME IN	TIME OUT

VISITOR LOG

DAY	NAME	TO SEE	TIME IN	TIME OUT

VISITOR LOG

DAY	NAME	TO SEE	TIME IN	TIME OUT

VISITOR LOG

DAY	NAME	TO SEE	TIME IN	TIME OUT

VISITOR LOG

DAY	NAME	TO SEE	TIME IN	TIME OUT

VISITOR LOG

DAY	NAME	TO SEE	TIME IN	TIME OUT

VISITOR LOG

DAY	NAME	TO SEE	TIME IN	TIME OUT

VISITOR LOG

DAY	NAME	TO SEE	TIME IN	TIME OUT

VISITOR LOG

DAY	NAME	TO SEE	TIME IN	TIME OUT

VISITOR LOG

DAY	NAME	TO SEE	TIME IN	TIME OUT

VISITOR LOG

DAY	NAME	TO SEE	TIME IN	TIME OUT

VISITOR LOG

DAY	NAME	TO SEE	TIME IN	TIME OUT

VISITOR LOG

DAY	NAME	TO SEE	TIME IN	TIME OUT

VISITOR LOG

DAY	NAME	TO SEE	TIME IN	TIME OUT

VISITOR LOG

DAY	NAME	TO SEE	TIME IN	TIME OUT

VISITOR LOG

DAY	NAME	TO SEE	TIME IN	TIME OUT

VISITOR LOG

DAY	NAME	TO SEE	TIME IN	TIME OUT

VISITOR LOG

DAY	NAME	TO SEE	TIME IN	TIME OUT

VISITOR LOG

DAY	NAME	TO SEE	TIME IN	TIME OUT

VISITOR LOG

DAY	NAME	TO SEE	TIME IN	TIME OUT

VISITOR LOG

DAY	NAME	TO SEE	TIME IN	TIME OUT

VISITOR LOG

DAY	NAME	TO SEE	TIME IN	TIME OUT

VISITOR LOG

DAY	NAME	TO SEE	TIME IN	TIME OUT

VISITOR LOG

DAY	NAME	TO SEE	TIME IN	TIME OUT

VISITOR LOG

DAY	NAME	TO SEE	TIME IN	TIME OUT

VISITOR LOG

DAY	NAME	TO SEE	TIME IN	TIME OUT

VISITOR LOG

DAY	NAME	TO SEE	TIME IN	TIME OUT

VISITOR LOG

DAY	NAME	TO SEE	TIME IN	TIME OUT

VISITOR LOG

DAY	NAME	TO SEE	TIME IN	TIME OUT

VISITOR LOG

DAY	NAME	TO SEE	TIME IN	TIME OUT

VISITOR LOG

DAY	NAME	TO SEE	TIME IN	TIME OUT

VISITOR LOG

DAY	NAME	TO SEE	TIME IN	TIME OUT

VISITOR LOG

DAY	NAME	TO SEE	TIME IN	TIME OUT

VISITOR LOG

DAY	NAME	TO SEE	TIME IN	TIME OUT

VISITOR LOG

DAY	NAME	TO SEE	TIME IN	TIME OUT

VISITOR LOG

DAY	NAME	TO SEE	TIME IN	TIME OUT

VISITOR LOG

DAY	NAME	TO SEE	TIME IN	TIME OUT

VISITOR LOG

DAY	NAME	TO SEE	TIME IN	TIME OUT

VISITOR LOG

DAY	NAME	TO SEE	TIME IN	TIME OUT

VISITOR LOG

DAY	NAME	TO SEE	TIME IN	TIME OUT

VISITOR LOG

DAY	NAME	TO SEE	TIME IN	TIME OUT

VISITOR LOG

DAY	NAME	TO SEE	TIME IN	TIME OUT

VISITOR LOG

DAY	NAME	TO SEE	TIME IN	TIME OUT

VISITOR LOG

DAY	NAME	TO SEE	TIME IN	TIME OUT

VISITOR LOG

DAY	NAME	TO SEE	TIME IN	TIME OUT

VISITOR LOG

DAY	NAME	TO SEE	TIME IN	TIME OUT

VISITOR LOG

DAY	NAME	TO SEE	TIME IN	TIME OUT

VISITOR LOG

DAY	NAME	TO SEE	TIME IN	TIME OUT

VISITOR LOG

DAY	NAME	TO SEE	TIME IN	TIME OUT

VISITOR LOG

DAY	NAME	TO SEE	TIME IN	TIME OUT

VISITOR LOG

DAY	NAME	TO SEE	TIME IN	TIME OUT

VISITOR LOG

DAY	NAME	TO SEE	TIME IN	TIME OUT

VISITOR LOG

DAY	NAME	TO SEE	TIME IN	TIME OUT

VISITOR LOG

DAY	NAME	TO SEE	TIME IN	TIME OUT

VISITOR LOG

DAY	NAME	TO SEE	TIME IN	TIME OUT

VISITOR LOG

DAY	NAME	TO SEE	TIME IN	TIME OUT

VISITOR LOG

DAY	NAME	TO SEE	TIME IN	TIME OUT

VISITOR LOG

DAY	NAME	TO SEE	TIME IN	TIME OUT

VISITOR LOG

DAY	NAME	TO SEE	TIME IN	TIME OUT

VISITOR LOG

DAY	NAME	TO SEE	TIME IN	TIME OUT

VISITOR LOG

DAY	NAME	TO SEE	TIME IN	TIME OUT

VISITOR LOG

DAY	NAME	TO SEE	TIME IN	TIME OUT

VISITOR LOG

DAY	NAME	TO SEE	TIME IN	TIME OUT

VISITOR LOG

DAY	NAME	TO SEE	TIME IN	TIME OUT

www.ingramcontent.com/pod-product-compliance
Lightning Source LLC
Chambersburg PA
CBHW080601030426
42336CB00019B/3281